The Purpose of this Book.

The pandemic of SARS-CoV-2 resulted from a naturally occurring corona virus that was modified to provide gain-of-function. This virus, dubbed CoVid-19 has resulted in more than 60-million infected individuals and 1.5-million deaths worldwide.

These deaths are the result of an Inflammothrombotic Response (ITR) to the virus and failure to treat the inflammatory and thrombotic consequences[1,2,3,4] in those people with impaired

---

[1] Fleming RM, Fleming MR. Proposed CoVid-19 Treatments: Lessons from the Inflammation & Cardiovascular Disease Theory. Coronavirus & Infectious Disease Research eJournal. Vol. 1, No. 164, October 20, 2020. September 17, 2020. Posted 19 October 2020). SSRN Preprints
https://ssrn.com/abstract=3694172
http://dx.doi.org/10.2139/ssrn.3694172
https://papers.ssrn.com/sol3/papers.cfm?abstract_id=3694172

[2] Fleming RM, Fleming MR. Fleming Inflammation and Cardiovascular Disease SARS-CoV-2 Proposed Treatment Protocol. Initial COVID Hydroxychloroquine Failure Responds to Interferon a-2b and Tocilizumab. J Clin Med Imag 2020;5(3):1-3.

immune system control, resulting from either a naïve immune system or individuals with increased immune responses resulting from comorbities. Comorbidities that affect more than half the world's population.

While vaccines that have been proven safe and effective can reduce morbidity and mortality, unsafe and ineffective vaccines can produce quite the opposite result.

The rush to develop these vaccines that (a) can neither stop infection since immunization does not actually prevent infection, and (b) will precipitate the very immune response that has already killed 1.5-million people, is myopic at best and poses a substantially greater potential threat to the health and

---

[3] Fleming RM, Fleming MR. Preliminary Results of Tocilizumab and Interferon a-2b Treatment of SARS-CoV-2. J Clin Med Imag 2020;5(3):1-4.

[4] Fleming RM, Fleming MR. Is there a treatment for SARS-CoV-2? Quantitative Nuclear Imaging finds Treatments for SARS-CoV-2. Research Square Preprints with 13 November 2020; DOI: 10.21203/rs.3.rs-106988/v1.

safety of people receiving the vaccine shot(s), as demonstrated with the H1N1 vaccine for Swine Flu.[5,6]

The Swine Flue vaccine was also approved by the FDA who assured us the Swine Flu vaccine was both safe and effective. It was neither and I took care of some of those patients who developed neurologic problems as a result of being vaccinated.

The guidelines for controlling SARS-CoV-2 were clearly violated as evidenced by the pandemic from Wuhan. The rush to develop and push these vaccines is a continued violation of protocols designed to produce safe and effective vaccines.

These violations raise serious ethical and medical questions that have not been answered.

---

[5] When the U.S. Government Tried to Fast-Track a Flu Vaccine. By: Christopher Klein. https://www.history.com/news/swine-flu-rush-vaccine-election-year-1976

[6] The Long Shadow of the 1976 Swine Flu Vaccine 'Fiasco'. By: Kat Eschner. https://www.smithsonianmag.com/smart-news/long-shadow-1976-swine-flu-vaccine-fiasco-180961994/

Approval of these vaccines by the FDA and other world health leaders and organizations can hardly be met with confidence given the track record of these agencies[7,8,9] and the potential conflicts-of-interest for those involved in the development of these vaccines.

All of this leaves me with many questions, just a few of which include: If the vaccine is so safe and effective, then why aren't the people making the vaccine getting vaccinated? Surely, if these vaccines are that good, safe and effective, then the workers producing the vaccines and the executives at these companies and their families, are critical to keeping

---

[7] Fleming RM, Chaudhuri TK. FDA Drug Recalls Epidemic. Re: Weight loss pill praised as "holy grail" is withdrawn from US market over cancer link. 21 February 2020. BMJ 2020;368:m705.

[8] Fleming RM, Chaudhuri TK. Should Big Pharma be Held Legally Liable for Misrepresentations made to the FDA? Acta Scientific Med Sci. 2019;Special Issue 1:05-07. DOI:10.31080/ASMS.2019.S01.0003.

[9] Fleming RM, Chaudhuri TK, McKusick A. The FDA, HHS, Sestamibi Redistribution and Quantification. Acta Scientific Pharmaceutical Sciences 2019;3(5):47-69. ISSN:2581-5423. https://www.actascientific.com/ASPS-Article- Inpress.php

the supply of vaccine coming to the rest of us. Why aren't they being vaccinated?

If the vaccines are that safe and effective, why aren't the world leaders getting vaccinated first, or for that matter the Federal Judges? Leaders lead, do they not? If you are going to force vaccination on anyone, then you should demonstrate the safety and efficacy by volunteering yourself and your family. If you are going to sit on the bench in a Courtroom and decide on punishment for people who refuse to be vaccinated, then you and your family should demonstrate that these vaccines are safe and effective.

The better question might actually be, Why are people NOT getting the types of treatments that have been shown to reduce the InflammoThrombotic Response (ITR) killing people, instead of pushing vaccines that will cause this deadly InflammoThrombotic Response?   Simply - WHY???

Operation Warp Speed – Who should be vaccinated?

As you have seen from the previous chapters, viruses enter and use the cells of our bodies to reproduce themselves. You have also seen that we can reduce the spread of respiratory viruses like CoVid-19 by staying away from others while we are infectious (not feeling well) and by washing our hands and the surfaces of objects we use, to reduce the spread of infection.

You have also seen that we have flipped the medical model on its head by quarantining the healthy and testing everyone to see if they have been exposed to the virus rather than testing those who may need immediate treatment and quarantining and treating only those infected, which would allow us to focus our time, money and resources, allowing us to treat those needing treatment sooner than later thereby saving lives.

This is not the only part of the medical model that has been flipped upside down. Usually we focus on treating people when they become critically ill – in this instance those who are either immune naïve or who have comorbidities placing them at increased risk.

Treatment of these individuals requires that we pay close attention to the InflammoThrombotic Response (ITR) precipitated as each person reacts to the virus. While the vast majority of people will kill CoVid-19 with their healthy immune system, those who die do so because of a failure to adequately control their immune response, forming blood clots and inflammation throughout their body including their lungs making it difficult and eventually impossible to breath.

Control and treatment of this immune response as shown in the following diagram is dependent upon whether we are addressing the pre-hospital, early acute cytotoxic or later adaptive humoral-antibody response to the virus as shown in the timeline. This time line shows what I believe to be the critical treatments at the critical times for SARS-CoV-2; aka CoVid-19, and the associated ITR response to Corona Virus Disease (CoViD).

Fleming SARS-CoV-2 Treatment Protocol

Pre-hospitalization	Hospitalization and Evaluation of SARS-CoV-2 severity on Day 1.	Rx Acute Innate T-cell Cytoxic Immune Response Beginning on Day 1.	Oxygenation Begin on Day 1.	Evaluate Treatment Response with FMTVDM on Day 3 after 72-hours of Rx.	Delayed Adaptive Humoral Immune & ITR Treatment. Day 3 immediately after FMTVDM.
Symptomatic or High-risk groups.	FMTVDM measurement of SARS-CoV-2.	Initiate Additional Treatment	Use incentive spirometry for Rx and measure of respiratory strength.	FMTVDM measurement to determine Rx effect.	Adjust Rx given FMTVDM results.
Begin HCQ, AZT or alternative (Primaquine & Clindamycin) to inhibit viral attachment and replication.	Begin pre-hospitalization Rxs if not already started.	Bronchodilator Rx with β-2 agonist.	With any compromise in ventilatory status begin PRONE positioning of patient.	(1) Improved. Cont Rx. (2) Stable. Add next level of Rx. (3) Deterioration. Change Rx.	If further Rx is to be added, select from (1) Tocilizumab & Interferon α-2β; (2) Primaquine, Clindamycin, Tocilizumab & Interferon α-2β, or (3) Methylprednisolone.
Begin Immune supportive Rx including Zn.	ECG and Rx any prolongation of QTc with Esmolol, K, Ca, & Mg.	Consider adding Primaquine 200 mg one time dose if not already given.	Consider supplemental oxygen and BiPAP.		Continue to aggressively address inflammatory and clotting disorders including efforts to get patient out of bed (chair, ambulate, etc.) to avoid further thrombotic and inflammatory problems.
Consider combination administration of interferon α-2β treatment with other agents - eg. Atrovent inhalers/ nebulizer; aminoquinoline; clindamycin.	Measure inflammatory & thrombotic markers and treat accordingly to address and prevent clotting and further uncontrolled inflammation.	Immediately add one of the three following treatment regimens to address InflammoThrombotic Response (ITR). (1) Tocilizumab & Interferon α-2β; (2) Primaquine, Clindamycin, Tocilizumab & Interferon α-2β, or (3) Methylprednisolone.	Prepare for V-V or V-A ECMO support.		Consider passive immunity with plasma with attention directed to potential associated clotting potential.
	Do NOT merely leave patient in bed (chair, ambulate, etc.).		If other measures fail consider ventilatory support with VT not to exceed 5 cc/kg IDBW. Extubate ASAP!		

This sequence of events will occur independent of whether the infection is acquired naturally or through immunization (vaccines) and failure to consider this in those being vaccinated could very well result in the same life-threatening consequences seen in those who acquire the virus naturally – potentially resulting in hundreds of thousands of deaths in addition to the inflammatory and blood clotting problems currently plaguing patients infected with this virus.

Rather than focusing on treating that which is killing people; viz. the InflammoThrombotic Response (ITR) to the virus, our focus to date – almost from day 1 – has been the development of a vaccine. While SARS-1 and MERS,[10] the two prior corona viruses discussed in Chapter 2, and HIV still do not have a

---

[10] Prompetchara E, Ketloy C, Palaga T. Immune responses in COVID-19 and potential vaccines: Lessons learned from SARS and MERS epidemic. Asian Pac J Allergy Immunol 2020;38:1-9.

vaccine, Dr. Fauci and others including Mr. Bill Gates - who may very well be qualified to address computer viruses but has no expertise that I'm aware of with biological viruses - have emphasized that without a vaccine, we cannot return to the lives we knew[11] before CoVid-19.

Coupled with the social isolation, loss of income, ever inflated numbers of people potentially infected, ostracization of those not complying with masks and "stay at home orders", discussions of immunity cards or other identifying methods, and threat of punishment via fines and shutting off of utilities[12] if not compliant, in addition to the imposed guilt of who you might infect and kill if you do not do what you are told to do, our world has come to

---

[11] https://www.realclearpolitics.com/video/2020/04/05/bill_gates_things_wont_get_back_to_normal_until_we_have_got_a_vaccine.html#!

[12] https://reason.com/2020/08/06/los-angeles-will-shut-off-peoples-utilities-for-hosting-parties-not-for-failing-to-pay-their-utility-bills/

resemble[13] something akin to that which we thought we had eradicated in the 1940s.[14]

Using the methods discussed in Chapter 3, the vast majority of individuals have been psychologically manipulated into a scenario where the cry for a vaccine has been louder than a cry for treatment for those already infected and hospitalized. If 911 taught us anything, people will trade freedoms and personal liberties for any promise of safety – even if that promise is unfounded or empty.

Almost as soon as the virus was recognized, Dr. Fauci announced the unconscionable progress being made in the development of a CoVid vaccine, while concerns were raised by others like Robert Kennedy Jr.[15] speculating on the involvement of

---

[13] https://www.nytimes.com/2020/06/30/style/mask-america-freedom-coronavirus.html
[14] https://www.businessinsider.com/home-depot-shoppers-fight-masks-white-power-comment-racism-2020-7
[15] https://www.youtube.com/watch?v=QLi6ZrFp6vQ

individuals and potential profit to be made by vaccine manufacturers as well as the impunity[16] protecting vaccine manufacturers should the vaccines cause harm to those injected with the CoVid vaccine product.

Similar concerns have developed in other countries including litigation by Rocco Galati, Esq.[17] in Canada. As a Canadian Constitutional attorney, Mr. Galati has expressed his concerns, concerns that have been echoed by others. In an email correspondence, Mr. Galati, Esq. stated:

> For me the whole vaccine issue, even prior to COVID-19, is really troublesome at its core when it comes to the successful propaganda that "vaccines are completely safe" (for everyone, all the time...)

---

[16] https://time.com/5585702/robert-kennedy-vaccines/
[17] https://omny.fm/shows/the-john-oakley-show/rocco-galati-legal-counsel-for-vaccine-choice-cana

when all the evidence shows, and is ADMITTED by the manufacturers, and every G-20 country except Russia and Canada by virtue of their vaccine compensation funds, that this is false.

This denial and suppression of the fact that those adversely affected are ignored, with the manufacturers and physicians being protected from lawsuits, removes any incentive to make vaccines safe for those who choose to take them, with the evolving reality that more and more jurisdictions are moving towards the elimination of the constitutionally protected right to informed medical consent.

The above concerns are magnified and amplified in the context of the COVID-19 frenzy, and irrational fears, where the pressure to global mandatory vaccination is that much greater and corrosively divisive.

With that pushed rush to reach a global mandatory market, we know and can reasonably predict, that the injury and death from these vaccines will reach avalanche proportions.

While Dr. Fauci and others have promoted the benefits of vaccine treatment, the data to date has not been as promising as hoped for[18,19,20] with multiple side-effects noted in preliminary studies of healthy individuals without comorbidities[21] and mounting evidence that the vaccines will be less than

---

[18] COVID-19: Not all patients develop protective antibodies. Medical University of Vienna. August 5, 2020.

[19] Zhu L, Yang P, Zhao Y, et al. Single-cell sequencing of peripheral blood mononuclear cells reveals distinct immune response landscapes of COVID-19 and influenza patients. Immunity. DOI: 10.1016/j.immuni.2020.07.009.

[20] Edridge AWD, Kaczorowska J, Hoste ACR, et al. Coronavirus protective immunity is short-lasting. 2020. DOI: 10.1101/2020.05.11.20086439

[21] Jackson LA, Anderson EJ, Rouphael NG, et al. An mRNA Vaccine against SARS-CoV-2-Preliminary Report. N Engl J Med 2020. DOI:10.1101/2020.05.11.20086439

effective, especially for those who are "obese" representing 40% of all adults.[22]

The development of a vaccine at pandemic speed[23] or Operation Warp Speed[24] as we have now come to call it misses the fundamental questions – What is the benefit of vaccinating everyone or more bluntly why are we actually vaccinating people, who will benefit from being vaccinated, and how did we manage to have the infrastructure in place to mass produce these vaccines and vaccinate the public?

The question of safety has already been addressed **but not in the way you would think it should be**. While the party line is that these vaccines will be safe, the truth is there is no incentive for the

---

[22] https://www.foxnews.com/health/potential-covid-19-vaccine-would-not-provide-same-level-of-protection-for-people-with-obesity

[23] Lurie N, Saville M, Hatchett R, Halton J. Developing Covid-19 Vaccines at Pandemic Speed. N Engl J Med 2020; May 21:1969-1973.

[24] https://www.hhs.gov/about/news/2020/08/07/fact-sheet-explaining-operation-warp-speed.html

drug manufacturers to make a safe vaccine because the vaccine manufacturers cannot be sued – even if the vaccine causes DEATH. According to U.S. Federal Law 42 U.S. Code §300aa–22 vaccine manufacturers cannot be sued for harm caused by their vaccines.

> (b) Unavoidable adverse side effects; Warnings.
> (1). No vaccine manufacturer shall be liable in a civil action for damages arising from a vaccine-related injury or death associated with the administration of a vaccine after October 1, 1988, if the injury or death resulted from side effects that were unavoidable even though the vaccine was properly prepared and was accompanied by proper directions and warnings. **42 U.S. Code §300aa–22**. Standards of responsibility

This same statutory law protects vaccine manufacturers from being sued if they fail to warn you of problems or potential problems with the vaccine.

> (c) Direct warnings.
> No vaccine manufacturer shall be liable in a civil action for damages arising from a vaccine-related injury or death associated with the administration of a vaccine after October 1, 1988, solely due to the manufacturer's failure to provide direct warnings to the injured party (or the injured party's legal representative) of the potential dangers resulting from the administration of the vaccine manufactured by the manufacturer. 42 U.S. Code §300aa–22. Standards of responsibility

The same litigation protection for the CoVid-19 vaccine manufacturers exists even in its experimental state, under "The Vaccine Act" and "The Public Readiness and Emergency Preparedness Act" (PREP Act), both passed by Congress to which the FDA and the HHS secretary – the people you thought were responsible for your safety – have participated in supporting the investigational exemptions under Sections 505(i) or 520(g) of the Food, Drug and Cosmetic Act.[25]

WHAT DO VACCINES REALLY DO?

Most people think that vaccines keep you from becoming infected by the virus or bacteria you are being vaccinated against. This is not correct.

The goal of a vaccine is to expose you to an infection in a "controlled" form – although if history has taught us anything, the best laid plans of mice

---

[25] https://www.law360.com/articles/1279847/covid-19-vaccine-developers-can-limit-liability-from-trials

and men go astray – as shown with the Swine Flu Vaccine[26] and the tainted polio vaccine.[27] The medical literature unfortunately has multiple reports of vaccine concerns.

Most vaccines are designed to elicit an antibody response to the infectious agent – in this case CoVid-19. The first question is what are you trying to produce an antibody to? Most of the vaccines under development for CoVid-19 are focusing on the obvious spike protein we talked about earlier in Chapter 1 that allows the virus to attach itself to our cells. The vaccine focus has interestingly been on the development of IgG and IgM antibodies and not the IgA[28] antibodies that

---

[26] https://www.smithsonianmag.com/smart-news/long-shadow-1976-swine-flu-vaccine-fiasco-180961994/
[27] https://www.washingtonpost.com/history/2020/04/14/cutter-polio-vaccine-paralyzed-children-coronavirus/
[28] https://www.sciencedirect.com/topics/medicine-and-dentistry/immunoglobulin-measurement

confer a protective response to infections occurring in the lungs and GI tract as discussed in Chapter 4.

There are other parts of the virus[343] some companies are working on, but the concept is the same – introduce some part of the virus you want our immune cells to make antibodies against with the hope that once the antibodies are made, you will also make memory B-cells (Chapters 4 and 5) that will remember the antibody and make more of the antibody once you get exposed to the virus from other people. <u>In other words, the assumption is that for the vaccine to have any potential benefit you must become exposed to CoVid-19 from someone spreading the virus.</u>

The most alarming of these vaccines may in fact be those using bacteriophages[29] used to inject

---

[29] Sulakvelidze A, Alavidze Z, Morris JG. Minireview Bacteriophage Therapy. 2001;45(3):649-659.

viral antigens directly into our cells. Ethical questions to this approach were raised in the 1960s and before, appreciating that the direct introduction of anything into human cells with the potential risks of influencing or perhaps altering our own genetic material might have more adverse outcomes than benefit, raising serious questions about safety – questions that no longer need to be addressed under the PREP Act and actions taken by the FDA and HHS as noted above.

Unfortunately for the vaccine manufacturers best laid plans, the duration of CoVid-19 IgM and IgG antibodies appear to be short lived.[352,30] What is being seen is some initial T-cell cytotoxic response[31] discussed in Chapters 4 and 5 of Unmasking CoVid[32].

---

[30] COVID-19 Antibodies Can Disappear After 2-3 months. https://www.webmd.com/lung/news/20200622/covid-19-antibodies-can-disappear-after-2-3-months.
[31] T-cell Responses to Coronavirus Vaccines Are In The Interest of National Security. https://seekingalpha.com/article/4367241-

The initial innate T-cell cytotoxic response is that part of the immune response that is activated in the first few days of any viral infection – including CoVid-19. This also explains why people with few or no symptoms have little evidence of antibody to CoVid-19.[33] Viral infections that are controlled by the initial cytotoxic response of our immune system will not survive long enough to generate a significant antibody response.

Since the goal of vaccinating people is to produce antibodies, or perhaps for CoVid-19, a sufficient T-cell response for cytotoxicity, the question is who would really benefit from such

---

t-cell-responses-to-coronavirus-vaccines-are-in-interest-of-national-security

[32] Fleming RM. Unmasking CoViD. Part 2. Finished 13 June 2020. With Literary Agent. Published online Amazon/Kindle 12 November 2020. ISBN 9798564029452.

[33] WHO warns that few have developed antibodies to Covid-19. https://www.theguardian.com/society/2020/apr/20/studies-suggest-very-few-have-had-covid-19-without-symptoms

vaccination and who might have problems as a result of being vaccinated.

The Benefits and Risks of CoVid-19 Vaccination in the Two Groups.

Most of us have been vaccinated for a variety of infections. I myself have been vaccinated for tetanus, diphtheria, pertussis, pneumococcus, hepatitis A and B, oral polio, measles, mumps and rubella. I have not been vaccinated against meningococcus, varicella (chickenpox), or human papillomavirus. I also have only been vaccinated once with the yearly "flu" vaccine and that was more than a decade ago. I am an allopathic physician, which means I am a M.D.

That being said, I am not an anti-vaccine physician – rather I was trained as a research scientist physician and I ask very specific questions regarding any health problem, directing my thoughts and questions to the diagnosis and treatment as demonstrated in this book. Consequently I ask very simple fundamental questions including why should someone be vaccinated for CoVid-19 and what are the consequences of that vaccination.

This approach not only emanates from my physician-scientist perspective but also from my physician's efforts to "do no harm." A responsibility I believe the FDA and HHS have abrogated with their support of their "warp speed approach" to vaccine development, and the politician's legislative legal approach of protecting vaccine developers by passing laws that protect vaccine manufacturers from legal liability for their vaccines. Billions have been spent for the development of vaccines. By comparison little money has been spent on developing or testing treatments except in those instances where Big Pharma will reap a significant financial reward for FDA approval of new drugs.

As should be obvious by now, our focus should be on diagnosing those who are symptomatic and need treatment. That treatment should be focused on the stage of the infection and control of our immune response to CoViD-19. That same attention needs to be focused on the use of a CoVid-19 vaccine. What does the vaccine do to the two different groups of people and how is this helpful or harmful.

I. Healthy Individuals.

As we have already seen, individuals with intact normally functioning immune systems may not even know they have been infected. For those who do, the classic symptoms associated with viral infections – body aches and pains, nasal discharge, elevated body temperature, fatigue, et cetera – in addition to some symptoms specific to this virus – e.g. loss of smell – present with symptoms that while uncomfortable are not life threatening.

These symptoms are in fact the body telling someone they have been infected and as you should know by now, means you are both able to spread the infection to other people – see Common Sense Chapter 3 – and you should stay at home not only to reduce the spread of the virus but to allow your body to recover.

Independent of whether you become exposed to the virus naturally or intentionally by a vaccine, this response will be the same with one exception. The vaccination itself has the additional risk of causing infection from bacteria on the skin[34] through which

---

[34] The skin is actually part of your immune system. It is designed to keep that which is outside of your body, out, and to keep that

the needle is stuck, as well as potential bleeding. There will of course be all the other side effects always present from vaccination, as already noted in the foot noted papers discussing the side effects already seen with CoVid-19 vaccines given to "healthy volunteers".

The cumulative result of this is that the vaccine will not prevent you from getting CoVid-19 from someone else. The goal is to hopefully shorten the amount of time it may take for you to react to the infection. The question based upon the preliminary studies is whether the CoVid-19 vaccine will actually make such a difference. If the vaccine only provides "some" antibody protection for "some" people for a couple months and the more likely benefit is from the

---

inside your body inside. By sticking a needle through your skin, you have just violated that first layer of protection. Certainly not a reason to not receive a vaccine if the vaccine provides a benefit. However, if there is no medical benefit, it raises the question of should you.

T-cell cytotoxic response, but your own T-cell cytotoxic response will kick in within a few days, and your symptoms will last roughly the same amount of time, where's the real benefit?

It is this group of people the preliminary studies are being done with and it will be this group of people they will use to sell the concept of everyone becoming vaccinated. If you want to show efficacy without safety issues, you select the people most likely to have no adverse effects and who can defeat the viral infection independent of whether the vaccine has any effect or not.

My suspicion and concern is that they will begin vaccinations using the first responders – those working in the hospitals, the EMS paramedics, and EMTs. Justifying this by saying these people - who will be selected by virtue of their being healthy individuals - need the "protection" and we owe it to those who have put themselves in harms way for the rest of us. This group, which is least likely to suffer inflammoThrombotic Reactions to the vaccine, as they are the ones least likely to experience an InflammoThrombotic Reaction to the virus itself, will then be used to promote the vaccination of everyone else, by telling us, that if those who put their very lives on the line to protect us were brave enough to volunteer to be vaccinated first, then the rest of us owe it to them to be vaccinated; using the same argument used for wearing masks and staying home.

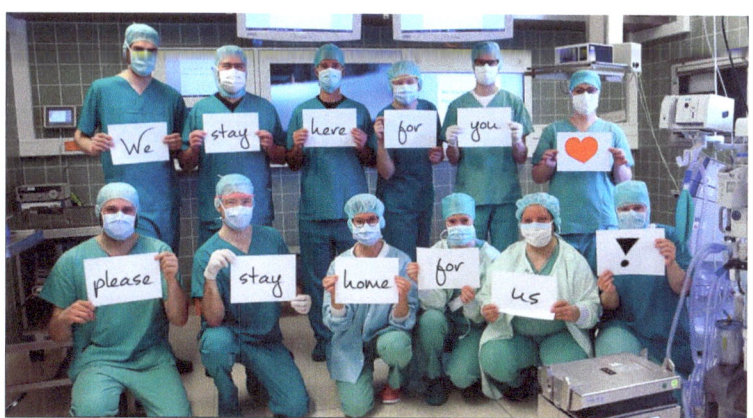

II. Those predisposed to an InflammoThrombotic Response (ITR).

These are the people who are either immune naïve or have the hyperimmune conditions associated with the elderly – including nursing homes or long term living conditions – heart disease, cancer, obesity, diabetes mellitus, high blood pressure, strokes or neurologic disease, kidney disease, and the other chronic inflammatory diseases plaguing modern society.

These are the individuals who when exposed to CoVid-19 develop an unrestrained InflammoThrombotic Response resulting in extensive inflammation and blood clots associated with hospitalization of so many and the deaths of hundreds of thousands of individuals.

Like those in the health group, vaccination will result in the activation of their immune responses; but unlike the healthy group, the activation of the immune response in these individuals following vaccination will have a different outcome. Instead of being exposed to the virus or part of the virus, and recovering in a few days, these people have already demonstrated that they will go on to develop an InflammoThrombotic Response leading to hospitalization, injury and death.

If the premise behind social distancing and masks is to reduce the spread of the virus to those most vulnerable to avoid their deaths, why would vaccinating this group of people make sense? You can't argue to prevent spread of the virus to this group and then argue to give the virus to this group. Remember, it's not the virus killing people but the InflammoThrombotic Response to the virus in those with impaired immune responses either resulting from a naïve, under or none developed immune system OR an over active immune system where further activation ignites[35] further health problems.

Summary

While there are many potential vaccines that could be used for any given infection including CoVid-19, the role of vaccination is to cause an immunologic response in the person vaccinated and that is exactly what will happen to people vaccinated for CoVid-19.

The premise being that once vaccinated and then exposed to the natural spread of CoVid-19, the vaccinated person will be able to mount an antibody response or perhaps T-cell cytotoxic response to the infection. However, the normal T-cell response mounted by healthy people happens within days with

---

[35] https://www.youtube.com/watch?v=mGyEvutNkvs&t=37s

or without vaccination. The very premise of this vaccination approach assumes that the virus will continue to circulate between people around the world. In those who are healthy and who would otherwise have no problems responding to CoVid-19, there is nothing added to the already functional immune system that will respond to the virus within days.

In the people with comorbidities, vaccination encourages the very InflammoThrombotic Response that has killed 1.5 million husbands, wives, sons, daughters, brothers, sisters, friends and neighbors. The vaccine does NOT prevent infection and it does not protect those most vulnerable from dying due to InflammoThrombotic Responses to CoVid-19. As such, the questions really are, *Who is vaccination really helping and Why the push to do it?*

www.ingramcontent.com/pod-product-compliance
Lightning Source LLC
Chambersburg PA
CBHW041945240526
45473CB00033B/519